RALPH VAUGHAN WILLIAMS

FOUR LAST SONGS

Words by Ursula Vaughan Williams

Arranged for SATB choir and piano by Jonathan Wikeley

OXFORD
UNIVERSITY PRESS

Great Clarendon Street, Oxford OX2 6DP,
United Kingdom

Oxford University Press is a department of the University of Oxford.
It furthers the University's objective of excellence in research, scholarship,
and education by publishing worldwide. Oxford is a registered trade mark of
Oxford University Press in the UK and in certain other countries

First published 2023

Impression: 1

ISBN 978-0-19-356416-9

Music origination by Ralph Woodward
Printed in Great Britain on acid-free paper by
Halstan & Co. Ltd, Amersham, Bucks.

Contents

Arranger's note

Of course, 'last pieces' are hardly conceived as such—rare is the composer who writes a final work and lays down their pen knowing they will not pick it up again. Ralph Vaughan Williams's *Four Last Songs* may be 'last', but it is likely they were not even thought of by him as a set: 'Menelaus' and 'Procris' were to be part of one cycle, and 'Hands, Eyes, and Heart' and 'Tired' as part of another.

That said, as a sequence the four songs offer a beautiful snapshot of two aspects of Vaughan Williams's writing. Vaughan Williams wrote for amateur choirs all his life. Like his younger colleague Britten he was able to write accessible music for the inexperienced singer that wears its learning lightly while losing none of its emotion. The middle two songs, 'Tired' and 'Hands, Eyes, and Heart', are simple and affecting, and in arranging them for unaccompanied choir I have tried to retain their simplicity.

'Procris' and 'Menelaus' show a different side to Vaughan Williams's writing. This is the Vaughan Williams of mystery and intense colour, of swirling mists and (occasionally dark) magic. The ever-shifting harmonies in these pieces offer both a challenge and an opportunity to the arranger. I have tried to harness some of the floating magic of Prospero in 'The Cloud-Capp'd Towers', and aimed to splash an extra dab of colour to Vaughan Williams's already fantastical piano score.

All four pieces would benefit from a nimble and flexible approach to choral singing. The pieces want, I think, to sound as artless and as effortless as possible—at times as if they were blowing about on the breeze—while at the same time the accompanying vocal lines in particular need to move exactly together, the singers always aware of what is happening in the other parts.

This arrangement was commissioned by the London Festival of Contemporary Church Music and first performed in 2022 to celebrate the 150th anniversary of the birth of Ralph Vaughan Williams.

Duration: *c*.10 minutes

This arrangement was commissioned by the London Festival of Contemporary Church Music and first performed in 2022 to celebrate the 150th anniversary of the birth of Ralph Vaughan Williams

Four Last Songs

1. Procris
(1958)

Ursula Vaughan Williams

RALPH VAUGHAN WILLIAMS
arr. Jonathan Wikeley

Pro - cris is ly - ing ___ at the wat - er - side,

15

wind_____ the thin trees lean towards the rush - es, the

18

pp

rush - es to the tide._____ She

pp murmured

Will not see, will not see,

pp murmured

Will not see, will not see,

pp murmured

Will not see, will not see,

pp

snow, with eyes so lit by love___ that ev - 'ry - thing

snow, with eyes so lit by love___ that ev - 'ry - thing

snow, with eyes so lit by love___ that ev - 'ry - thing

snow, with eyes so lit by love___ that ev - 'ry - thing

burned, flowed,___ grew, blos - somed,___ moved on

burned, flowed,___ grew, blos - somed,___ moved on

burned, flowed,___ grew, blos - somed,___ moved on

burned, flowed,___ grew, blos - somed,___ moved on

2. Tired
(1956)

*taken from a mixture of sopranos and altos, always with a mind to the overall balance.

Pochissimo animando

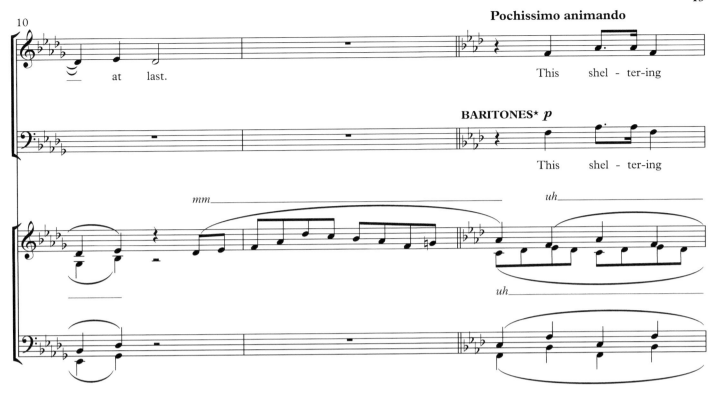

at last.

This shel - ter-ing

BARITONES* *p*

This shel - ter-ing

mm ____ *uh* ____

uh ____

mid - night is our meet-ing place,____ no pas - sion or des -

mid - night is our meet-ing place,____ no pas - sion or des -

uh ____

uh ____

uh ____

uh ____

*taken from a mixture of tenors and basses, always with a mind to the overall balance.

-pair or hope di - vide_____ me from your side.

-pair or hope di - vide_____ me from your side.

uh_____

uh_____

uh_____

uh_____

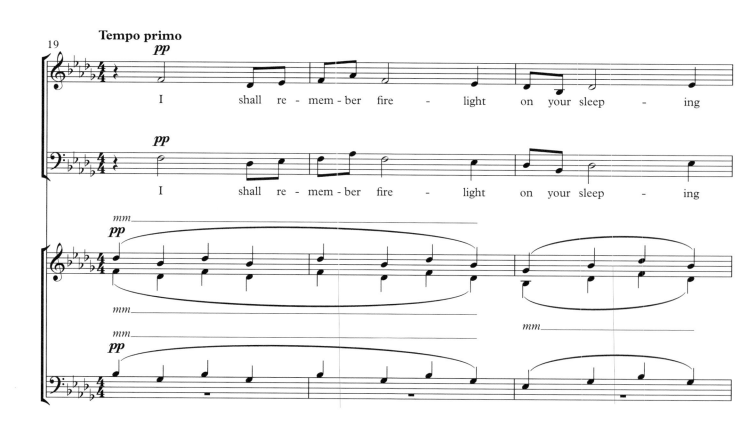

Tempo primo

pp

I shall re - mem - ber fire - light on your sleep - ing

pp

I shall re - mem - ber fire - light on your sleep - ing

*mm*_____

pp

*mm*_____ *mm*_____

*mm*_____

pp

3. Hands, Eyes, and Heart
(?1956)

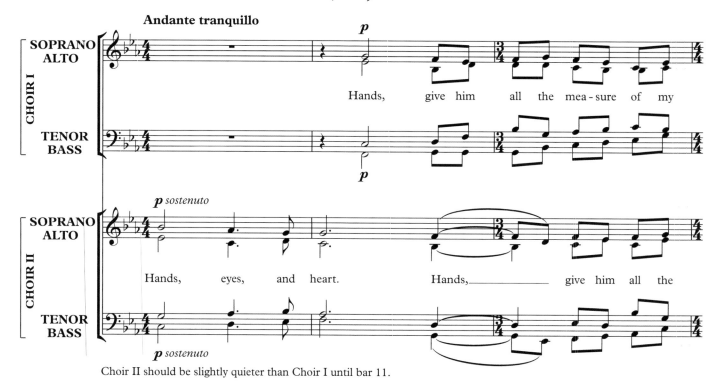

Choir II should be slightly quieter than Choir I until bar 11.

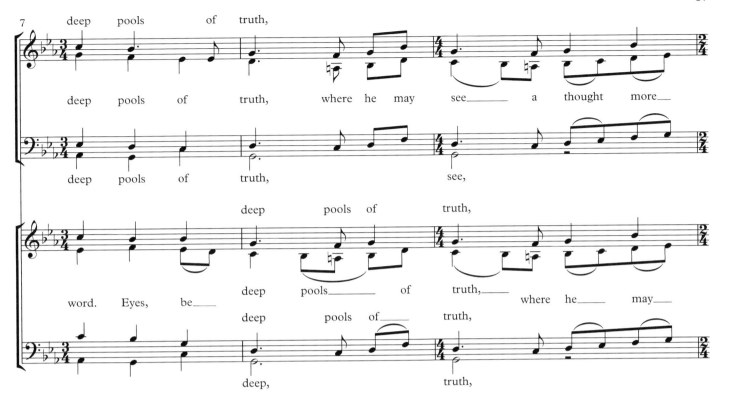

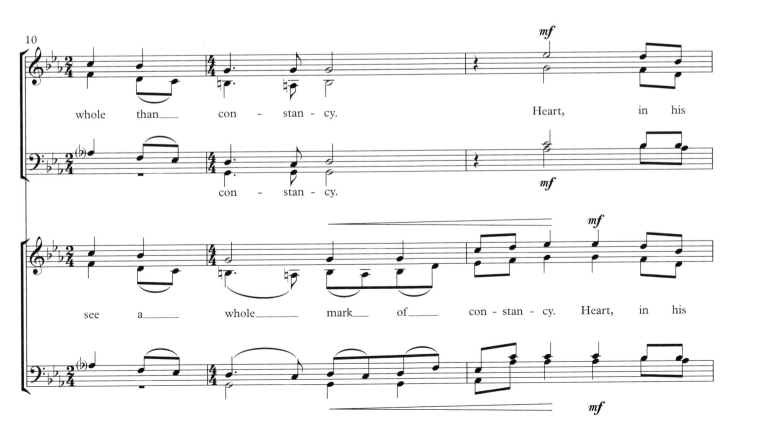

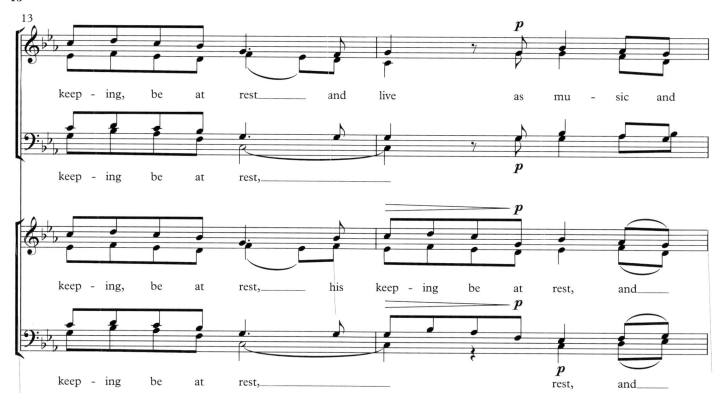

keep - ing, be at rest____ and live as mu - sic and

keep - ing be at rest,____

keep - ing, be at rest,____ his keep - ing be at rest, and____

keep - ing be at rest,____ rest, and____

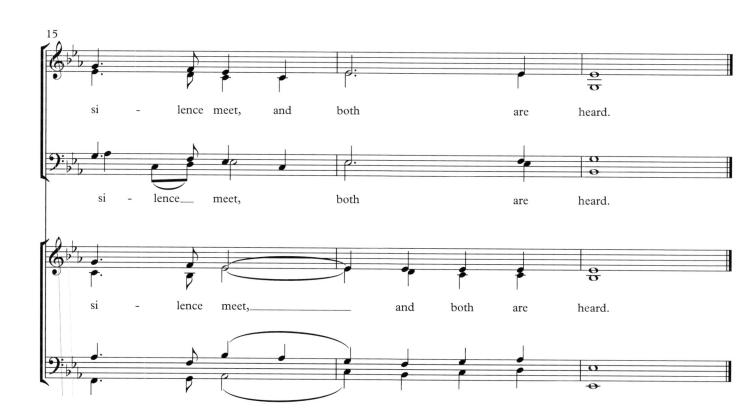

si - lence meet, and both are heard.

si - lence____ meet, both are heard.

si - lence meet,____ and both are heard.

4. Menelaus
(1954)

grow.

Home - sick

wan - der, you will come home

T.B. whisper 'will you come home?',
each singer at a different speed.

to a home more

to a home, a home more

and swal - lows nest be - low

lin - - tel and eaves:

there lamps are kin - dled for you, they will burn till you

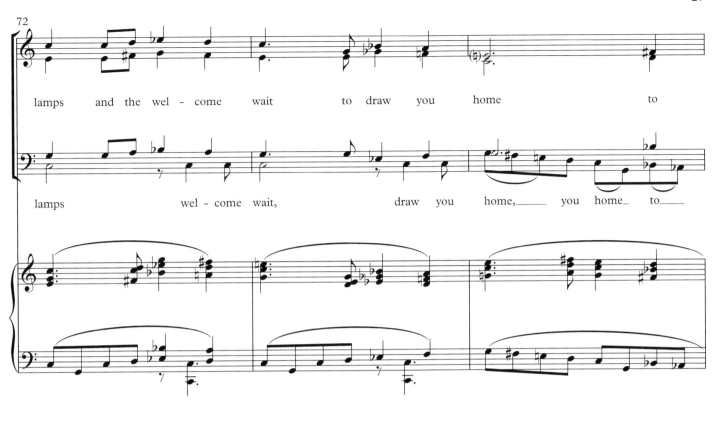

lamps and the wel - come wait to draw you home to

lamps wel - come wait, draw you home, you home to

rest._____ You__ shall come home_____ and__ love_____

rest._____

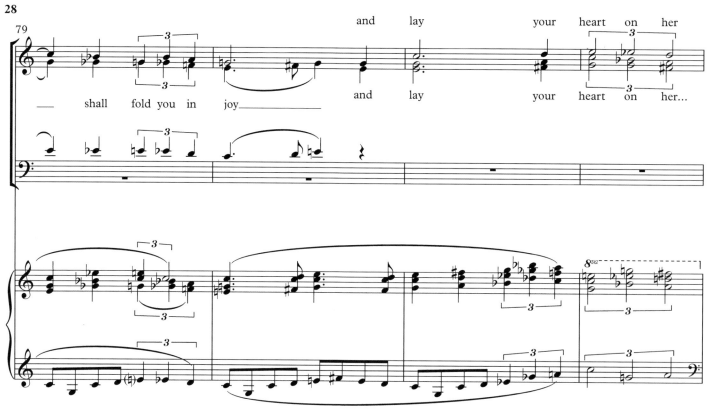